THE LIGHT OF THE GURU

ACKNOWLEDGMENTS
*Our thanks go to Peggy Bendet for writing and compiling the text,
Cheryl Crawford for design, and to all those others
who offered their service with love.*
– *Richard Gillett*

Quotation on p.36 by kind permission of Destiny Books,
Inner Traditions International Ltd., Rochester, VT.

Published by the SYDA Foundation®
PO Box 600, 371 Brickman Road
South Fallsburg, New York 12779-0600, USA

Copyright © 1994 SYDA Foundation. All rights reserved.
First published 1994. Second printing 1994
No part of this book may be reproduced or transmitted in any form or by any
means electronic or mechanical, including photocopy, recording or information
storage and retrieval system, without permission in writing from SYDA Foundation,
Permissions Department, PO Box 600, 371 Brickman Rd.
South Fallsburg, New York 12779-0600, USA

(Swami) MUKTANANDA, (Swami) CHIDVILASANANDA,
GURUMAYI, SIDDHA MEDITATION and SIDDHA YOGA
are registered trademarks of SYDA Foundation®.
Printed in the United States of America

ISBN 0-911307-32-X

THE LIGHT OF THE GURU

The Celebration of Guru Purnima

A SIDDHA YOGA PUBLICATION
PUBLISHED BY SYDA FOUNDATION

The Tradition of Siddha Yoga

Siddha Yoga is a path of spiritual unfoldment that is inspired by the grace and guidance of an enlightened Master, known as a Siddha Guru.

A Siddha Guru is one who has the power and knowledge to give others the inner experience of God. Through the transmission of grace, known as Shaktipat initiation, the Siddha Master awakens a seeker's inner spiritual energy. Having walked the spiritual path to its final goal, Siddha Gurus dedicate their lives to helping others complete the same journey.

Swami Chidvilasananda is a Siddha Guru. Since early childhood, she has been a disciple of the Siddha Master Swami Muktananda Paramahamsa (1908-1982). It was he who invested Swami Chidvilasananda with the knowledge, power, and authority of the ancient tradition of Siddhas.

During his lifetime Swami Muktananda became adept at many of the classical paths of yoga, yet he said his spiritual journey did not truly begin until Bhagawan Nityananda, one of the great saints of modern India, awakened him to the experience of the supreme Power within himself.

Bhagawan Nityananda chose Swami Muktananda as his successor and directed him to take Shaktipat initiation and the timeless practices of yoga to seekers everywhere. The path Swami Muktananda taught, which introduced the wisdom and disciplines of the ancient sages to the modern world, came to be known as Siddha Yoga. Swami Chidvilasananda, who is also known as

Gurumayi (literally, "one who is absorbed in the Guru"), continues in her Guru's tradition. Swami Chidvilasananda travels the world offering the teachings of the Siddhas and Shaktipat initiation to genuine seekers everywhere.

Through Siddha Yoga and its principal practices of meditation, chanting, contemplation, and selfless service, thousands of people from many different traditions and cultures have discovered within themselves the source of lasting happiness and peace: the awareness that we are not separate from God.

Introduction

A great mystery surrounds the relationship between the spiritual Master and the disciple. All traditions honor the enlightened teacher, the one who has traversed the inner path and returned to guide others on their own journey. In India, the bond with the Master is especially treasured, and many great beings have testified to the Guru's unique power to connect us to our own experience of God.

Yet the true understanding of the Guru arises when we experience the Guru not only as a great teacher, but as the inner principle of grace, the subtle power which returns an individual to his or her divine source.

Guru Purnima, the full moon day dedicated to the Guru, honors both the form of the Guru and this hidden power of grace.

Celebrated throughout India, it is one of the most important holidays of the year in Siddha Yoga Meditation ashrams and centers. On Guru Purnima, the Guru's blessings are especially abundant. It is a day that can bestow, on one who enters fully into it, an experience of the deepest meaning of the Guru's grace. By understanding the profound symbolism of this day, its history and inner significance, we can move beyond the outer level of the celebration and open ourselves to receive its gift: the experience of the light of grace within ourselves.

— Swami Durgananda

Guru Purnima, the celebration of all celebrations, is the day devoted exclusively to the Guru.

All days and nights are nothing but the pulsation of the Guru's Shakti.

And yet, O my beloved Guru Muktananda, Guru Purnima is that day and night when even the moon reveals its full luster, when all days and nights have reached their culmination and are in suspension, awaiting a glimpse of their own Master.

— Swami Chidvilasananda
Ashes at My Guru's Feet

It is endless, absolutely endless, what the Guru has given — and what he can still give. This is grace! Somehow you feel he has offered everything; he has given himself, and what could transcend that? But there is more, there is more, and there is still more. The Guru's grace never ends.

— Swami Chidvilasananda
  speaking on *Guru Purnima* 1986

The first full moon in the Indian month of Ashadha, which falls in June/July in the Western calendar, is a time of celebration for devotees of the Guru. It is Guru Purnima, the full moon of the Guru, the day set aside to honor the spiritual Master, to offer gratitude for his grace.

Just as the full moon sends rivers of light to the earth without being diminished by its gift, so the Guru invites the world to drink from the inexhaustible font of inner knowledge. The Guru's beneficence is portrayed in a Vedic mantra, *Om purnamadah purnamidam…* The meaning is this: That which is whole, that which is perfect, comes only from perfection; and yet when the perfect is taken from perfection, still only perfection remains.

*I offer myself to the Guru.
Why? My eyes were filled with darkness.
I saw the world through the darkness
 of my own eyes,
And everything looked so dark.
Then my Guru applied
 the lotion of grace to my eyes,
 and the darkness was removed.
I saw the entire world as light,
And nothing but light.*

—Brahmananda

From the Guru flows perfect grace, which can transform whomever it touches. The function of the Master's grace is to return us to our own innate perfection: we can know our own true worth and experience the indescribable light that lies within us. The saint Kabir said the moon and the sun shone within his body, but until he received the grace of the Master, he was blind to them. Kabir sang, "It is the mercy of my true Guru that has made me know the unknown."

To be given the passport to this inner paradise is to receive the greatest gift in all of God's creation, a gift that the devotees of the Guru strive in some small way to repay, particularly on the first full moon of July.

The moon itself has great significance for this auspicious time. In India, where the land is consecrated and rivers are holy, the moon

A true Guru awakens the inner Shakti of a disciple and makes him revel in the bliss of the Self. This is what the Guru really is: the one who awakens the inner Shakti Kundalini through Shaktipat, who sets the divine Shakti in motion in man's body, who gives instruction in yoga, who bestows the ecstasy of knowledge and the joy of divine love, who teaches detachment in action and grants liberation in this very lifetime.

— Swami Muktananda

is thought of as the bearer of nectar and the source of inspiration. The entire ninth book of the *Rig Veda*, one of the most ancient of all scriptures, is devoted to the praise of Soma, or Chandra, the deity identified with the moon. In *Play of Consciousness*, Swami Muktananda's account of his spiritual experiences, he describes how in meditation he visited the world of the moon, Chandraloka. This is one of the inner realms that can be experienced by those who explore the depths of their inner being. Swami Muktananda, or Baba as he is known, said Chandraloka was suffused with a soft and gentle light and the dwellings were made of silver and gold. Years later, when one of the U.S. astronauts who had landed on the moon visited Baba, they spoke about their respective journeys to what they agreed was a powerful and sacred place.

The scriptures speak of the sixteen phases of the moon, from the finest sliver of the dark

The relationship of the Guru and his disciple should be honored as the torch of light leading to God.

— *Yoga Vasishtha*

nights to the luminous orb that lights up the earth with its silvery brilliance. According to legend, the moon was one of the twenty-seven teachers of the forefather of all Gurus, Shri Dattatreya, who saw by watching its continuous waxing and waning that only its form was altered by time. He understood that just as the essential nature of the moon remains the same through all phases, so the essence of all forms in the universe is unchanging.

Baba Muktananda used to describe the moon as the "deity for restlessness" because he said its calming light has the power to bring the mind to rest. The cooling rays of the moon can take the yogi to a subtle realm beyond the heat of the passions, opening an inner world of beauty and light. In this respect, there is no phase of the moon more powerful than the culmination; the full moon, or *purnima*.

The full moon is a time when people recite sacred mantras, bathe in holy rivers,

When God was distributing the full moons, he gave the most perfect one to the Guru.

— Swami Muktananda
  speaking on Guru Purnima 1980

and make offerings to fulfill lofty purposes. In India each of the full moons of the year is dedicated to the worship of a particular deity, to the attainment of a particular power or virtue. The greatest of the purnimas — the time when the full moon is fullest and its power the most expanded — is said to be the full moon of July, Guru Purnima.

Guru Purnima honors all spiritual Masters, past and present. It is associated with Dattatreya, who is traditionally seen as the supreme Reality taking the form of the Guru, and with Shankaracharya, the great sage who was the propounder of the philosophy of Vedanta. Another name for the holiday is *Vyasa Purnima*, for according to legend, it was in honor of the great sage Vyasa that the first Guru Purnima was celebrated.

Veda Vyasa, as he is often called, is credited with writing down many of India's most fundamental scriptures. He is said to have

Shankaracharya [the Guru] is the full moon, showering his cooling nectar on those who are overwhelmed by the fierce heat of the sun in the desert of the world.

— Morning and Evening Arati, 15

compiled the four Vedas; recorded the eighteen minor and eighteen major Puranas, including the *Shiva Purana* and the *Shrimad Bhagavatam*; and dictated what is possibly the longest epic tale ever written, the *Mahabharata*. In the *Mahabharata*, Maharishi Vyasa is the Guru for both the Pandavas and their opponents, the Kauravas; he is the sage who makes appearances throughout the story to offer compassion, a boon, or a word of advice. When he was asked to write down this immense tale, it seemed an impossible task, even for Vyasa, and so he asked Lord Ganesha to act as his scribe. Ganesha agreed to write down Vyasa's words only if the sage did not pause once he had begun to speak, and Vyasa set a condition of his own: that Ganesha would not write down anything he didn't understand. According to legend, each of them kept his agreement — while Ganesha pondered Vyasa's words, the sage had time to compose further verses —

He is worthy of being called the holiest of the holy. The mere sight of him commands respect, and in his company even a deluded person becomes absorbed in God. Religion lives through his words, the sight of him produces the highest attainment, and he takes constant pleasure in heavenly bliss. When we remember him, his greatness is imparted to us. Let it be so.

—Jnaneshwari, 6.102-104

and the monumental work took only two and a half years to complete.

Once the *Mahabharata* had been set down in writing, Vyasa's disciples appealed to the sage for some way to thank him for the divine wisdom he had imparted to them. This is a classic wish: the blessings that flow from the spiritual Master are so extraordinary, the disciple is left with a sense of indebtedness impossible to repay. There was really nothing that Vyasa's disciples could do to express the depth of their gratitude to their Guru—and yet out of love for him they longed to make an offering.

Vyasa told his disciples they could set aside one day a year to honor the Guru with gifts and festivities. He added, "On this day any gift offered to the Guru with love and devotion will reach me." Therefore on Guru Purnima when we honor our own Guru as an embodiment of divine wisdom, we are also

The Guru is a burning flame.
Even if thousands of flames are lit
    from it, it is not affected.
When you want to light a candle,
    you bring together a flame
    and an unlit wick.
As you bring them closer and closer,
    a leap occurs, and the wick is lit.
The moment for you to become
    something will come sooner
    or later, and then there need
    only be a leap.
Therefore, have satsang at the Guru's feet.
It is the Absolute who exists in the
    form of the Guru.

—Swami Muktananda

honoring the ancient seer of divine wisdom, Veda Vyasa.

In India, where Guru Purnima occurs during the rainy season, there seems to be a natural concurrence between the seasons of the year and the seasons of *sadhana*, of the spiritual path. After the blazing fire of the hot season comes the relief of the cooling rains. And, in the same way, the auspicious moon of Ashadha provides the crucial transition from the desert of outer life to the cooling rain of Guru's grace and the deliberation of contemplative inner life.

The monsoon is named *chaturmasya*, which literally means "four-twelfths" or "four months." The monsoon is often half that length; the name *chaturmasya* is used because of a Vedic tradition by which time is considered twice as long during certain periods of austerity — in other words, time is twice as valuable when used in such an auspicious way.

Compared with other stones, he is the touchstone. Compared with other liquids, he is nectar.... If by chance a diamond were found in a lump of camphor and water fell upon it, wouldn't the diamond emerge with its form intact? In the same way, although this person may seem to be an ordinary person, the weaknesses of nature are unknown to him. Sins avoid him for fear of their lives. Just as a serpent leaves a burning sandalwood tree, similarly, desires pass by the person who knows the Lord.

—Jnaneshwari, 10.74-78

And chaturmasya, particularly for monks, is a time devoted to the austerity of sadhana — to meditation, chanting, and scriptural study. During the monsoon wandering ascetics, *sadhus*, and *sannyasins* are expected to engage in intense spiritual practices and to remain in one place through the entire season.

Traditionally, traveling sadhus would stop in whatever town or village they happened to reach on Guru Purnima, and as they stated their *sankalpa*, their intention, to do austerities for the time of the rains, they would ask the local residents for permission to stay. Usually this was freely granted; it is a householder's *dharma*, his responsibility, to support sadhus during this holy time, and great merit is said to accrue to those who follow these scriptural injunctions.

The sage Vyasa is thought to have begun writing the *Brahma Sutras*, which contain the fundamental teachings of Vedanta, on Guru

*To him who has the highest love
 for God, and for Guru as for God,
To that great soul the truths taught here
 shine forth in all their glory.
Yes, to that great soul
 they shine forth in all their glory.*

— Shvetashvatara Upanishad, 6.24

Purnima, and so it is traditional for sannyasins to spend the day studying this great scripture. Through the rest of chaturmasya, they might read any of the other classical texts — the Upanishads, the *Bhagavad Gita*, the *Vedantasara*, among them. It also is customary at this time to eat lightly; fruit and milk are considered appropriate to the season. And it is an especially powerful time to do continuous repetition of one's Guru mantra or of the *mahavakyas*, the great Upanishadic dictums.

The *pujas*, or rites of worship, performed on Guru Purnima involve traditional symbols of auspiciousness: flowers, incense, *kumkum*, turmeric, rice, and, most essentially, a flame, representing the light of knowledge. Mantras are sung from the ancient texts, and *abhishek*, a ritual bathing, is offered to the Guru's sandals.

The sandals, or feet, of the spiritual

Dhyana mulam guror murtih
puja mulam guroh padam
Mantra mulam guror vakyam
moksha mulam guroh kripah

The root of meditation is the Guru's form.
The root of worship is the Guru's feet.
The root of mantra is the Guru's word.
The root of liberation is the Guru's grace.

—*Guru Gita, 76*

Master have great mystical significance. They are said to contain the whole of his power, not just symbolically but literally. Because Shakti, subtle energy, naturally flows from the head to the feet, the Guru's feet contain the greatest concentration of his power. One of the great mysteries of the spiritual Master is that his feet, as well as the power they contain, can actually be experienced from within by the disciple. Many great beings have recommended that seekers keep their minds focused on the Guru's feet as a way of opening to grace. It is a practice as unfailing and mysterious as serving the Master or chanting God's name. In Siddha Yoga Meditation ashrams, the *Shri Guru Paduka Panchakam*, "Five Stanzas on the Sandals of Shri Guru," is recited daily. This is followed by the *Guru Gita*, an ancient text which itself describes the power of remembering the Guru's feet.

*For the gift of knowledge
approach a Master,
one who is both learned
in the scriptures
and established in Brahman.*

— *Mundaka Upanishad, I: 2.12*

On the auspicious day of Guru Purnima all spiritual practices performed have heightened power. According to Vedic astrology, each of the purnimas is connected to a particular star or stars, called *nakshatras*, and to their attributes and qualities. At the time of a full moon, the sun and moon are in opposition, with the moon receiving full illumination from the sun and the earth receiving full illumination from the moon. Thus any star influencing the moon or sun at this time is in the right position to pour its qualities onto the earth.

During the purnima in the month of Ashadha, the moon is moving under a star named Purva Ashadha, known in Western astrology as Pelagus, Sigma, or Vega Sagittarii. According to the Vedas, this star is the provider of water — fitting for the time of

Guru Purnima is a symbol of the perfection of the Guru. On the full moon day, the moon showers purest nectar. So on Guru Purnima day, the Guru showers the nectar of supreme bliss.

— Swami Muktananda

the monsoon. In Sanskrit the word for water is also associated with "life," and "life" is not just the life of the body but also the life, or attainment, of spirit. On this purnima, too, the sun is opposite Betelgeuse, the star whose deity is Lord Shiva, the primordial Guru. So on this day, the moon showers the earth with the qualities needed for spiritual life, and the sun showers the earth with the grace of the primordial Guru.

The opposition of the sun and moon has another significance: the moon is "full" because it is fully facing the sun, the source of light, and in the same way the Guru is aligned with the supreme source of light; he is fully facing God. The Sanskrit word for full moon, *purnima*, has its root in the word *purna*, which is defined as "full, abundant, rich, fulfilled, finished, complete, entire, contented, strong, capable, able, accomplished, perfect." The Guru is one who is

*I have met my Sadguru; all of
    my sorrows have departed.
The doors to my inner being have been
    flung open.
The fire of knowledge has been lit within
    my body.
All the millions of karmas have
    been burnt.
The five thieves who were robbing me
    day and night have left me of their
    own accord.
Even without a lamp, I am illumined.
I do not know where the darkness
    has gone....
Kabir says, Listen, fellow sadhu!
The Light has merged into the Light.*

— Kabir

"perfect" in that he is fulfilled within himself and content with whatever life offers. The Guru has immersed himself in the abundance of inner love; he has completed the spiritual journey and is able to lead the disciple on the path, inspiring the disciple to realize his own inborn perfection.

Baba Muktananda once said, "Guru Purnima literally means 'perfect Guru.' But not only is the Guru perfect; we are perfect. If only the Guru is perfect, what's the use of the Guru?... The meaning of Guru Purnima is that the Guru makes *you* perfect."

The nature of the bond between the Guru and the disciple is symbolized by the very syllables of the word *guru*. The first syllable, *gu*, signifies "darkness," and the second syllable, *ru,* is "light." So the term *guru*, which is itself a great mantra, describes the functions of the Guru, the dispeller of darkness, the revealer of light.

As darkness is destroyed at the very sight of a lamp, so is ignorance destroyed at the very sight of the holy Guru.

— Kularnava Tantra, 3.16

One of the beauties of the Sanskrit language is that it offers opportunities to explore many nuances of meaning. The primary etymology of the word *guru* is "heavy." There is no way to measure the weight, the significance, of the Guru in the life of a spiritual seeker. All analogies pale before the reality of the Guru. We may compare the Guru to the perfection of the full moon, but as the great saint Jnaneshwar wrote, "The moon is only full at times, while these beings are eternally perfect."

The journey to the Guru is a very significant undertaking. In the years when Baba's Guru, Bhagawan Nityananda, lived in the village of Ganeshpuri, the surrounding area was little more than a jungle and the roads leading to it were rudimentary. At the best of times, the trip from Bombay to the Guru's ashram was an adventure. During the Guru Purnima celebration one year, Gurumayi spoke about

The Guru is not this body. The Guru is the grace-bestowing power of God. The Guru is Shakti, divine power, and not vyakti, an individual being. The Guru has great power. He can take souls who are burning in the fire of agitation of this world to a place where there is only coolness and shade. By reaching that place, an individual soul loses his separate existence and merges into God.

— Swami Muktananda
   speaking on *Guru Purnima* 1981

what it was like to make this journey to see Bhagawan Nityananda on that auspicious day, in the rainy season, when often roads would be flooded and bridges washed out. Encountering these obstacles, devotees would abandon their cars and set off on foot, wading through water, sliding through mud, often for miles. "And finally, sometimes two days later," Gurumayi said, "without food, without any shower—but wet!—you would arrive for the Guru's sweet *darshan*, something you really wanted."

On Guru Purnima, however, there would be a sea of other people who had also arrived for Bhagawan Nityananda's darshan, and a long line would snake through the tiny village of Ganeshpuri. "Then," Gurumayi said, "six days after you had left home— no exaggeration!—having stood in the line for darshan day in and day out, you would get to go inside the hall where Bhagawan

A true Guru is one who just by the power of his touch can show a seeker the inner Truth and make the purest love arise within him.

If you have gained the Guru, then there is nothing more to gain.

If you have received the Guru's knowledge, then there is no more knowledge to receive.

If you have experienced the Guru's blessings, there is no more joy to be experienced.

Any true disciple would offer himself to his Guru in a very humble manner on this day and consider it his greatest fortune.

— Swami Muktananda
speaking on Guru Purnima 1982

Nityananda was. And when you got inside — he would turn his back on you."

One might think that people would be overcome by sadness then, that they would start feeling that they were undeserving or unworthy. But something else would happen.

"There would be a divine vision," Gurumayi said. "There would be no more body, no more place. You would see that which you had never before seen; you would hear that which you had never before heard. You would be totally outside of body consciousness. And then Bhagawan Nityananda would make this incredible sound, all the way from the navel region, very deep within, as if it was coming from the depths of the ocean. And that sound would bring you back to your senses, and you would know it was time to move on."

People would walk outside and sit, lost in ecstasy, having received within themselves what they had come for.

*The full moon is veiled by the clouds;
  until the clouds move away,
  the moon will not be visible.*

*When your clouds move away,
  the Inner Moon will appear.
You will see in this Moon of Wisdom
  the light of a million moons...*

— Bengali poet

*P*erfection lies in the inner light, the inner world. Three and a half centuries ago when the Italian astronomer Galileo Galilei first looked at the moon through a telescope, he noted that there appeared to be mountains and craters and seas, the features that create the appearance of "the man in the moon," or, in the East, "the mark of the hare." This contradicted the understanding of the time that all heavenly bodies were perfect and smooth. Yet the inner moon, the inner light, is perfect, and its radiance surpasses that of the moon that rises and sets. In India, during Guru Purnima, the monsoon clouds are often very thick and the moon is altogether invisible. To devotees of the Guru, however, being able to see the moon is not essential: they have the grace to be able to turn within themselves and find the true meaning of the full moon of the

The Moon of Mystery

There is a center of power in the middle of the sahasrara, at the crown of the head; below that is the moon; let the wise contemplate this.

—Shiva Samhita, 5.145,147

Guru, to experience the inner radiance. "This light," Gurumayi once said, "is the experience of love, the experience of Truth, of God, of the Self within. This light is so powerful. It gives life. It contains everything for us."

As a seeker progresses on the spiritual path, the energy known as Kundalini, the sacred spiritual power, ascends in the subtle system through seven centers, called *chakras*. Within the topmost spiritual center in the crown of the head, the *sahasrara*, there is a light, called "the moon of Consciousness" or "the moon of mystery." The great beings have described this effulgence, shining in the inner sky across an ocean of pure energy. "This is the glorious moon of the Lord," Gurumayi once said, "your own inner Self. It shines silvery white, with no blemish, ever pure, ever serene."

The *Guru Gita*, the text on the glory of the spiritual Master, describes this effulgence

Contained in the sahasrara is the full moon, without the mark of the hare, resplendent as in a clear sky. It sheds its rays in profusion, and is moist and cool like nectar. Inside it, constantly shining like lightning, is a triangle and inside this, again, shines the Great Void which is served in secret by all the gods.

— Shat Chakra Nirupana, 41

in the crown of the head in great detail, saying that within the light is a triangle and within that are "the Guru's lotus feet." The vision of this mystical form of the Guru's power, of this symbol of reverence, is an aspect of the highest spiritual experience. Saints sing of the gentle rain of nectar that pours from the inner moon, of the radiance of eternal moonlight that is itself music and love. Kabir says, "There love songs resound, and light rains in showers; and the worshiper is entranced in the taste of heavenly nectar."

The luminous inner world, portrayed in veiled terms in the esoteric scriptures, is revealed from within by the grace of the spiritual Master. One of the most extraordinary discoveries of this experience is that what may have once seemed to be poetic hyperbole — references to the "darkness" of ignorance being lifted, and the "light" of knowledge shining forth — turns out to be simple

Many are those Masters who are honored and served, resplendent with Consciousness and discrimination. But, O Goddess, it is hard to find that Master who [himself free of ego] can destroy the egos of others. It is through him that revelation is communicated, through him that all things are accomplished, through him that, freed of ego, one recognizes oneself in one's essential purity.

— *Hamsabheda Tantra*

description. Wisdom comes in the form of light; it is the light itself that teaches.

One woman who was partially blind was longing to see Gurumayi during a talk in the Shakti Mandap in South Fallsburg several years ago. The woman was craning her neck and squinting her eyes to catch a glimpse of the one who had made such a difference in her life. All she could manage to make out was a blur. Finally she had to give up. She sat back and closed her eyes... and immediately her vision was filled with a soft, scintillating light. The radiance suffused her entire being. It was her inner being. She knew it. And also she knew, with an intuition that was rock firm, "This is the Guru."

Baba Muktananda used to say, "The Guru is not just this individual being; he is that light. The Guru is the one who is in the center of that triangle in the sahasrara.... The real Guru is the vibrating divine bliss

Baba Muktananda was a perfect Guru. Nature gave his life her fullness. Baba was born on a full moon, and when he took mahasamadhi, the full moon was his witness. Guru Purnima, the Guru's moon, the largest moon of the year, was a holiday that Baba loved very much. And because of his love for his Guru, he took every occasion to celebrate this day of the perfect full moon with great joy and fullness of heart.

— Swami Chidvilasananda

which throbs in the center of the sahasrara. Only when one becomes aware of that inner Guru does one love the outer Guru and understand that the outer is really the inner. Only when you worship the inner Guru will you really worship the outer Guru."

This is the true perfection of Guru Purnima: the reverence we pay to the Sadguru on this holiest of days is a means of recognizing the divinity that lies within us. And when we honor our innermost Self in this way, we are fully honoring the Guru.

Om purnamadah purnamidam
Purnat purnamudacyate
Purnasya purnamadaya
Purnamevavasisyate

*Om. That is perfect. This is perfect.
From the perfect springs the perfect.
If the perfect is taken from the perfect,
the perfect remains.*

— *Upanishads*

For information about books by Swami Muktananda and
Swami Chidvilasananda and about editions in translation write to
Siddha Yoga Meditation Bookstore, 371 Brickman Road,
PO Box 600, South Fallsburg, NY 12779-0600, USA.
(914) 434-2000 ext.7757

You may learn more about the teachings and practices of
Siddha Yoga Meditation by contacting:
SYDA Foundation
371 Brickman Road, PO Box 600,
South Fallsburg, NY 12779-0600, USA
(914) 434-2000

or

Gurudev Siddha Peeth
PO Ganeshpuri
PIN 401 206
District Thana
Maharashtra, India